MOTORMANIA

RACING CARS

ROB COLSON

WAYLAND
www.waylandbooks.co.uk

First published in Great Britain
in 2020 by Wayland
Copyright © Hodder and Stoughton, 2020
All rights reserved

Series editor: John Hort
Produced by Tall Tree Ltd
Designer: Jonathan Vipond

HB ISBN: 978 1 5263 1262 4
PB ISBN: 978 1 5263 1263 1

Wayland
An imprint of Hachette Children's Group
Part of Hodder and Stoughton
Carmelite House
50 Victoria Embankment
London EC4Y 0DZ

An Hachette UK Company
www.hachette.co.uk
www.hachettechildrens.co.uk

Printed and bound in China

Picture Credits
t-top, b-bottom, l-left, r-right, c-centre, front cover-fc,
back cover - bc
fc Toyota, jamesteohart/Shutterstock, 1, 2t Daimler AG, 2b, 7t
carpouzi, 2c, 25b Chevy Racing, 4b Mark W Lucey/Shutterstock,
4–5 Biblioteque national de France, 5t Library of Congress, 5b
betto Rodrigues/Shutterstock, 6 cristiano barni/Shutterstock,
7cl, 7cr, 7b SpazGenev/Shutterstock, 8t, 9tr Maserati Spa, 8b, 9br
Bob Cullinan/Shutterstock, 9bl Timitrius, 10–11, 10b, 11l, 11r
Daimler AG, 12, 13bl Action Sports Photography/Shutterstock,
13tl Jeremy Christensen/Shutterstock, 13tr James Pierce/
Shutterstock, 13br National Automotive History Collection,
Detroit Public Library, 14–15t Phillip Abbott/LAT for Chevy Racing,
14–15b Honda, 15t Steve Fecht for Chevy Racing, 16–17, 16b, 17t,
17b Toyota, 18c, 18b, 19t, 19br Toyota, 19bl Studio BKK/
Shutterstock, 20–21 Paul Stringer/Shutterstock, 21t Popperfoto
via Getty Images/Getty Images, 21b Fluky Fluky/Shutterstock,
22–23, 23b, 24–25 Action Sports Photography/Shutterstock, 22b
Phillip Rubino/Shutterstock, 23t Getty Images, 25t Alan Marler/
HHP for Chevy Racing, 26tl Manamana/Shutterstock, 26b, 27t,
31 Nacho Mateo/Shutterstock, 27b Volkswagen AG, bc, 28
Oskar Schuler/Shutterstock, 29t Frederic Legrand - Comeo/
Shutterstock, 29br Cineberg/Shutterstock

Every attempt has been made to clear copyright. Should
there be any inadvertent omission, please apply to the
publisher for rectification.

CONTENTS

MOTOR RACING

Ever since the motor car was invented in the 1880s, people have raced cars. The earliest motor races were events run by enthusiastic amateurs, who competed in their own cars. Later, manufacturers developed new kinds of racing car, pushing the limits of technology.

Cars line up on the grid for the 1934 French Grand Prix at the Autodrome de Linas-Montlhèry circuit, near Paris.

FIRST RACE

The first organised motor race was held in France in 1894. Twenty-one cars competed in the race, which took place over a 126-km course from Paris to Rouen in France. The winner, a Peugeot driven by Frenchman Albert Lemaître, completed the course in just under 7 hours.

In their design, early cars resembled the carriages pulled by horses. They were fitted with engines that generated 3 hp (**horsepower**), meaning that it would take three horses to pull the carriage with the same power.

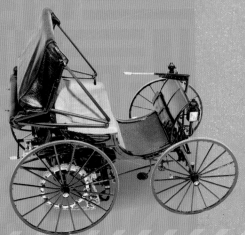

The first cars had a top speed of about 20 km/h.

THE BIG PRIZE

By the early 20th century, races known as Grand Prix (French for 'Big Prize') were being held. Cars raced around circuits formed from public roads or on purpose-built tracks. In the 1930s, new racing cars were developed specially for Grand Prix races. The fastest could reach top speeds of more than 400 km/h.

ROUND THE WORLD

The longest motor race in history took place in 1908. Six cars lined up for the start of the race in New York on the east coast of the USA. They drove across the USA, then caught a steam boat to Russia and drove to Paris, France. Three cars completed the race, driving a total of 16,700 km in just under six months of racing.

Competitors line up for the start of the 1908 round the world race.

RACING FOR ALL

American autocross is a form of racing that allows anybody with a car to compete. Instead of driving against each other, competitors complete timed laps of the track, which is marked out with traffic cones. There are various classes for different kinds of car.

This Chevrolet Corvette Stingray is competing in an autocross class for powerful **muscle cars**.

RACE
THE MONACO GRAND PRIX

Formula 1 (F1) is the ultimate racing competition, with races held across the world. Raced around the streets of Monte Carlo on the Mediterranean coast, the Monaco Grand Prix is the most glamorous event in the F1 calendar, and the race that every driver wants to win.

NARROW CIRCUIT
The course winds through narrow streets with sharp turns, making this a true test of driver skill. Overtaking is difficult, which makes qualifying very important. Qualifying takes place the day before the race. Drivers complete a series of timed laps of the course, and the times determine their place on the starting grid.

MONACO LEGEND

Brazilian driver Ayrton Senna (1960–1994) won the Monaco Grand Prix a record six times, including five wins in a row from 1989 to 1993. A three-time F1 World Champion, Senna is considered one of the greatest drivers in history. Tragically, he was killed in a crash during the 1994 San Marino Grand Prix. Following his death, the sport introduced new safety measures to protect drivers.

CIRCUIT DE MONACO

LOCATION:
Monte Carlo

CIRCUIT LENGTH:
3.337 km

MOST WINS:
6 – Ayrton Senna

FIRST HELD:
1929

RACE DURATION:
78 laps

LAP RECORD:
1 minute 14.26 seconds
(Max Verstappen, 2018)

NOUVELLE CHICANE
A chicane is a double bend in the track. At Monaco, the cars enter the Nouvelle Chicane at high speed. They have to brake sharply, and this is one of the few places where a driver can overtake a rival.

FAIRMONT HAIRPIN
Drivers drop to 50 km/h at the slowest corner in Formula 1. The section is so tight that teams adapt their cars' suspension and steering just for the Monaco race.

TUNNEL
Drivers pass into the Tunnel at one of the fastest points on the circuit. This is a potentially dangerous section, as the cars lose some of the **downforce** that keeps them safely on the track.

CLASSIC F1
MASERATI 250F

Formula 1 racing started in 1950. The first decade of the competition was dominated by Italian manufacturers, such as Maserati. The Maserati 250F raced between 1954 and 1958.

MASERATI 250F

WEIGHT:
670 kg

ENGINE:
2.5 litre, 6 cylinders

POWER:
240 hp

TRANSMISSION:
5-speed

TOP SPEED:
290 km/h

SIMPLE DESIGN

Formula 1 cars in the 1950s looked very different from today's high-tech machines. With its simple tube-shaped **chassis** and open cabin, the Maserati 250F offered little protection to the driver. It took a lot of courage to take it up to full speed at nearly 300 km/h. Crashes were frequent, and 15 drivers were killed in the first decade of F1 racing.

Fangio (see right) on his way to victory at the 1957 German Grand Prix.

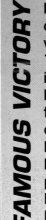

FAMOUS VICTORY

Legendary Argentinian driver Juan Manuel Fangio won five F1 titles in the 1950s. He won his last title in 1957 in a Maserati 250F. Fangio's final win came in the German Grand Prix at the Nürburgring circuit. Finding himself 50 seconds behind the leader after a pit stop had gone wrong, Fangio stormed to victory, breaking the lap record 10 times to take the lead on the final lap.

FRONT ENGINE LAYOUT

The 2.5-litre engine sat at the front of the 250F. From 1959 onwards, new F1 cars placed the engine behind the driver, which gave the cars better balance, making them easier to **handle**. The Maserati 250F found itself outpaced by these mid-engine cars, and by 1961, all drivers had switched over to the new design.

MODERN F1

MERCEDES-AMG F1 W10

Racing on tricky courses with sharp turns, F1 cars are designed to take corners at breathtaking speed. Each year, the cars must meet strict new rules regarding engine size, body shape, fuel capacity and safety features. Mercedes were the most successful constructor in F1 from 2014 to 2018. This is the car they prepared for the 2019 season.

*The engine sits behind the driver, covered by the **aerodynamic** body.*

The wings are tilted at an angle to produce enough downforce but not too much drag.

DOWNFORCE

To take corners at high speed without skidding, F1 cars need to create lots of downforce. Most of this is generated by the front and rear wings. As air passes over the wings, it presses down on them, helping the tyres to grip the track when taking corners. However, this also increases the force of **drag**, which slows the cars down. On fast tracks, wing size is reduced to increase speed on the long straights.

*Under F1 rules, all four wheels must be uncovered. They are made from magnesium **alloy**.*

TECH POINT

A T-shaped 'halo' wraps around the open cockpit just above the level of the driver's helmet, protecting the head in the event of a crash. The halo is now a compulsory part of all F1 cars. It must be able to withstand a weight of more than 12 tonnes. Made from lightweight titanium, the halo weighs about 12 kg. Manufacturers experiment with its shape to make the halo as aerodynamic as possible.

F1 W10

WEIGHT:
743 kg

0–100 KM/H:
2.1 seconds

ENGINE:
1.6 litre, 6 cylinders

TOP SPEED:
413 km/h

CONTROL CONSOLE

The steering wheel is also the driver's control console, allowing them to perform every function without taking their hands from the wheel. It has 25 buttons and switches, controlling gear changes, brake settings, power adjustors and communications with the pit lane. On a typical lap of a race circuit, which is about 4 km long, the driver will change gear about 50 times.

Gear shift paddles

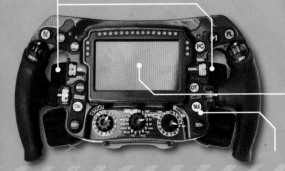

LCD Display screen

Radio

RACE
THE INDY 500

IndyCar is the premier open-wheel car racing championship in the US. This annual series is named after its most famous race, the Indianapolis 500, widely known as the Indy500. '500' refers to the race length of 500 miles (805 km).

Crowds of more than 300,000 people pack the stands at the Indianapolis Motor Speedway.

INDIANAPOLIS MOTOR SPEEDWAY

LOCATION:
Indianapolis, Indiana

FIRST HELD:
1911

CIRCUIT LENGTH:
4 km

LAP RECORD:
37.895 seconds
(Arie Luyendyk, 1996) average speed of 382.2 km/h

RECORD RACE TIME:
2 hours, 41 minutes, 18.4 seconds
(Arie Luyendyk, 1990)

MOST WINS:
4 – AJ Foyt, Al Unser, Rick Mears

400 m turn

200 m straightway

FAST TRACK

The 4-km track is a rectangular oval shape. A field of 33 cars race one another over 200 laps. Each 90-degree turn is banked, so the cars take them without losing much speed, and they never drop below 350 km/h. Driving at such speeds is deemed too dangerous in wet conditions, so the race is postponed when it rains.

The Indianapolis Motor Speedway was built in 1909.

INDY STAR

American driver Danica Patrick (born 1982) made history in 2008 with her victory in the Indy Japan 300 race. It made her the first woman to win an IndyCar race. Patrick competed in IndyCar for seven seasons before switching to NASCAR (see pages 24–25). She returned to IndyCar in 2018 for her final race in the Indy500, but she crashed out on lap 68.

PIT STOP

During the race, cars come into the pits to change tyres and refuel. A highly trained pit crew of six engineers changes all four tyres, refuels and makes adjustments to the wings in less than 10 seconds. A slow pit stop can lose a driver the race.

1 km straightway

Pit lane

FIRST 500

The first Indy500 race was held in 1911. It was won by Ray Harroun, driving the Marmon Wasp (right), a car he had designed himself. Harroun completed the distance in 6 hours, 42 minutes, 8 second. More interested in engineering than driving, Harroun immediately retired from racing after his victory.

DALLARA DW12

INDYCAR

In the IndyCar Series, all teams use the same DW12 chassis, made by Italian manufacturer Dallara. The DW12 was designed in 2012, to be used for nine years of racing.

AERODYNAMICS

An aero kit is fitted around the chassis of the car. This is made up of lots of adjustable parts designed to produce downforce to keep the cars on the road when cornering, while also allowing them to cut through the air along high-speed straights. The parts can all be adjusted to suit each of the 15 circuits in the IndyCar season, which are a mix of tight, winding tracks and high-speed ovals.

WINGS
These provide downforce.

TECH POINT

The core of the Dallara chassis is designed for maximum driver safety. The driver sits inside a safety cell, surrounded by energy-absorbing foam. Drivers also wear a HANS (Head And Neck Support) device, which prevents skull fractures in high-speed accidents.

As all drivers use the same chassis, IndyCar races are a test of pure driving ability and the races are closely fought.

DW12

ENGINE:
2.2 litre, 6 cylinders

WEIGHT:
717 kg

POWER:
575 hp (speedways),
675 hp (road courses)

TOP SPEED:
386 km/h

0–100 KM/H:
3.5 seconds

ENGINE AND FUEL:
The cars are fitted with standard engines, supplied either by Chevrolet or Honda. The fuel capacity is limited to 70 litres, which makes the refuelling strategy a vital part of a race. During the Indy500, cars need to refuel at least six times.

ENGINE COWLING
This is a slick, aerodynamic cover for the engine.

SIDEPODS
These protect the sides of the car. They also help to cool the engine, provide an aerodynamic shape and protect the driver in case of a side impact.

RACE

THE 24 HOURS OF LE MANS

In endurance races, cars complete as many laps as possible over a fixed time period. Endurance races include separate classes of cars racing at the same time: Le Mans Prototypes (LMPs), made just for endurance racing; and Grand Tourers, which are modified road cars. At the Le Mans 24-hour race in France, teams of three drivers take turns racing the car for a full day.

CIRCUIT DE LA SARTHE

THE MULSANNE STRAIGHT
The Mulsanne Straight is a straight-line section of the course that used to be 6 km long. Chicanes were added to slow cars down along the straight in 1990, as LMPs were reaching dangerous speeds of more than 400 km/h.

La Sarthe circuit combines a race track with public roads that are closed off for the race.

Almost a third of the race is held at nighttime. For many drivers, this is a special period in the race that requires total concentration. Some sections have no lights around them, making it feel like you are driving in a tunnel. Overtaking is especially difficult at night. The LMPs are up to 40 km/h faster than the Grand Tourers, and the drivers of slower cars have to check for the headlights of a faster car approaching from behind.

F1 TO LE MANS

Spanish driver Fernando Alonso (born 1981, left) won back-to-back Formula 1 Championships in 2006 and 2007. In 2017, he turned his hand to endurance racing. Alonso won the 24 Hours of Le Mans at his first attempt, in 2018 alongside teammates Kazuki Nakajima (centre) and Sébastien Buemi (right).

FIRST HELD:
1923

TRACK LENGTH:
13.626 km

LAP RECORD (DURING THE RACE):
3 minutes 17.475 seconds
(André Lotterer, 2015)

MOST WINS:
9 – Tom Kristensen

CROWD SAFETY

For many years, only an earth bank separated spectators from the track. This changed after disaster struck in 1955. French driver Pierre Levegh's car was knocked off the track, and burning shrapnel flew into the crowd. Levegh was killed instantly, and 83 spectators also died. Crowds are now kept safely away from the track.

WEC
TOYOTA TS050

In 2016, Japanese manufacturer Toyota unveiled its new LMP, the TS050 Hybrid. This revolutionary car features a combined petrol engine and electric motor. After a difficult first season, the car has dominated the World Endurance Championship.

The engine and battery are behind the driver.

RACING RULES

With their wide, low chassis, large rear wings and roaring engines, LMP cars are unmistakable on the track. Unlike open-wheel cars such as F1 cars, racing rules require all mechanical parts to be covered by bodywork. They are aerodynamically shaped to produce maximum lap times with minimum fuel consumption, as the fuel used in a race is limited. All cars must conform to a strict set of rules and dimensions.

Toyota's two cars finished first and second in seven of the eight races in the 2018–2019 season.

The chassis is a lightweight carbon-fibre monocoque.

TS050

TECH POINT

The car is a **hybrid**, meaning that it is powered by a petrol engine and an electric motor. The batteries for the motor are charged by energy recovered when the car brakes, giving the driver the option to add extra power when needed. To add even more power, the engine is fitted with a twin-turbo. Turbo chargers reuse energy from the exhaust. The exhaust fumes are forced down a narrow tube, where they spin a **turbine**. The turbine is linked to a compressor, which sucks air into the engine, helping the fuel to burn.

ENGINE:
2.5 litre, 6 cylinders

WEIGHT:
875 kg

POWER:
1,000 hp

TOP SPEED ON THE TRACK:
340 km/h

0–100 KM/H:
2 seconds

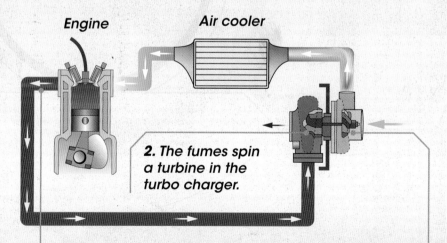

Engine

Air cooler

2. The fumes spin a turbine in the turbo charger.

1. Exhaust gases from the engine are forced into the turbo charger.

3. Powered by the turbine, the compressor sucks air into the engine.

KARTS

Many Formula 1 champions, including Ayrton Senna, Michael Schumacher and Lewis Hamilton, started their racing careers behind the wheel of a kart. Superkarts are the fastest karts of all. With their light weight and superb handling, karts are a true test of driving skill.

SHORT BUT FURIOUS

Superkarts are the biggest and fastest karts. The karts only have small fuel tanks, so races are short. They are held over distances of about 40 km and are completed in about half an hour.

SUPERKART

WEIGHT :
200 kg (including driver)

ENGINE:
250 cc, 2 cylinders

POWER:
90 hp

TOP SPEED:
250 km/h

0-100 KM/H:
3 seconds

STARTING YOUNG

Kart races are split into classes for different age groups. The youngest racers are just eight years old. These are the potential stars of the future. They drive small 60 cc Cadet karts with a top speed of about 80 km/h. Lewis Hamilton (pictured) won his first Cadet Championship aged just nine.

Sixty or more Superkarts line up at the start of a race, but there is plenty of room for overtaking and the races are always action-packed.

TECH POINT

Kart drivers need to be skilled engineers. Some make their own karts from special kits, or even build a kart from scratch using a lawnmower engine! Kart racers need to check and adjust their karts correctly before each race.

TOP FUEL
DRAGSTERS

These monsters are the biggest, fastest and noisiest racing cars of all. They have the best acceleration of any racing machine. Racing side-by-side on a straight 305-metre track, they hit the finish line in under 4 seconds, reaching speeds of more than 500 km/h. Blink and you'll miss it!

HIGH-SPEED THRILLS

Drag races, in which cars or motorbikes line up next to one another for a sprint race, have been popular ever since motor vehicles were invented. Top fuel races, with the very fastest cars, were first officially organised in the US in 1963.

At most events, cars race two at a time, but at the Four-Wide Nationals in Concord, North Carolina, there are four lanes.

BURNOUT
Before the start of the race, drivers perform a burnout. They spin the wheels on the spot, creating billowing clouds of smoke. This gets the tyres up to racing temperature. It also creates a lot of noise. A top fuel dragster is as loud as a jet plane!

TOP FUEL DRAGSTER

ENGINE:
8.2 litre, 8 cylinders

POWER:
at least 8,000 hp

WEIGHT:
1,057 kg

LENGTH:
up to 8 metres

0–100 KM/H:
0.8 seconds

RECORD SPEED:
541.66 km/h
(Tony Schumacher, 2018)

MULTIPLE CHAMPION

In the late 1970s, Shirley Muldowney (born 1940) was the undisputed champion of Top Fuel. Defying opposition from some men who didn't want a woman to race, Muldowney won three World Championships between 1977 and 1982.

SPECIAL FUEL

Top fuel dragsters take their name from their fiery fuel. The fuel is made from a mix containing 90 per cent nitromethane. This mix catches fire very easily. It is dangerous, but explosively powerful, producing up to 2.3 times more power than petrol. During a race, the car burns up to 80 litres of fuel.

EXTREME FORCE

The races put enormous strains on the drivers' bodies. At the start, the acceleration creates a force of up eight times stronger than gravity. Drivers wear neck supports to stop their heads from flying back. At the end of the race, the cars need parachutes to help them to brake.

CHEVROLET CAMARO ZL1

Stock car races are competitions for ordinary road cars that have been modified for the track. The biggest stock car competition in the world is the NASCAR Cup Series, which is contested in a series of 26 races held across the USA.

CHAMPION MODEL

Chevrolet are the most successful manufacturer in the NASCAR Cup Series. Their current car is the Camaro ZL1. While it looks like the ordinary production model from the outside, the NASCAR version has been built very differently.

OVAL SPEEDWAY
Most NASCAR races are held on oval speedways such as the Charlotte Motor Speedway, with banked corners that allow the cars to maintain hair-raising speeds for the whole race.

TECH POINT

The first part of a stock car to be built is the **roll cage**. This is made of thick metal tubing and it protects the driver in a crash. The body is built around the roll cage using handmade metal panels. These are shaped to make the car as aerodynamic as possible, as it will need to maintain speeds over 300 km/h on the fast oval tracks.

CAMARO ZL1

DURABLE ENGINE

The engine is specially designed for racing, with durable parts that can withstand high temperatures and pressures. The engine needs to maintain 10,000 rpm (revs per minute) for the whole race, and it is tested thoroughly before it is fitted to the car.

ENGINE:
5.8 litre, 8 cylinders

WEIGHT:
1,565 kg

POWER:
850 hp

The tyres are filled with pure nitrogen instead of air. This is done to minimise moisture inside the tyre, which can cause unwanted increases in pressure at high temperatures.

WRC
FORD FIESTA WRC

Rallies are races in which cars drive against the clock over rough surfaces, including gravel, dirt, snow and ice. The top rally competition is the World Rally Championship (WRC), a series of 14 three-day events. The cars are highly modified production cars, such as the Ford Fiesta WRC.

Flat side skirts add downforce.

CO-DRIVER
The co-driver sits in the passenger seat. They carry a series of race notes, and use these to navigate each stage. Co-drivers also need the skills of a mechanic, as they may be required to change a wheel or perform minor maintenance during the race.

FORD FIESTA WRC

ENGINE:
1.6 litre, 4 cylinders

WEIGHT:
1,190 kg

POWER:
300 hp

TRANSMISSION:
Six-speed gearbox and four-wheel drive

A TEST OF SKILL

The WRC has a set of strict rules to ensure that races are close and a good test of driving skill. Overall car weight is restricted, and advanced electronic control systems are forbidden. The engine must not be larger than 1.6 litres and the power is limited to 300 hp.

SHOCK ABSORBERS

Rally cars need a tough suspension to survive the bumps, jumps, holes and rocks they drive over during a race. The wheels are fitted with sturdy shock absorbers that are three times the diameter of the shock absorbers on a road car.

WINNING TEAM

French driver Sébastien Ogier (born 1983) has dominated the World Rally Championship in recent years, winning it six times in a row from 2013 to 2018. He won his first four titles in Volkswagen Polo R WRC before switching to a Ford Fiesta WRC. Ogier (pictured, right) has raced with the same co-driver, fellow Frenchman Julien Ingrassia (left), since 2006. A trusted co-driver plays a crucial role in rallying success.

FORMULA E
SPARK GEN2

Formula E is a single-seater racing series for electric cars that has run since 2014. All the drivers use cars with the same chassis, meaning that races are always closely contested. A new car was unveiled for the 2018–2019 season. The Spark SRT05E, or Gen2, is built by Spark Racing Technology and Dallara.

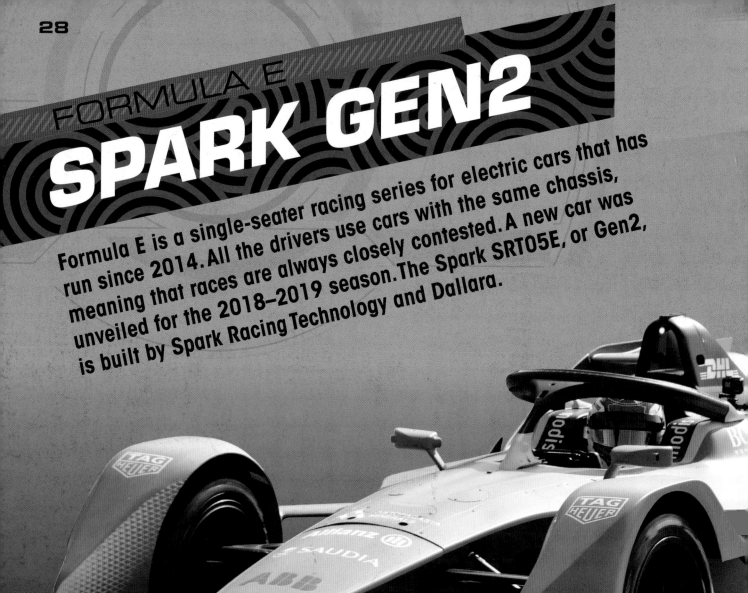

ELECTRIC POWER

One of the biggest technological challenges of electric cars is to make a long-lasting battery. The Spark Gen 2 has batteries with twice the energy storage capacity of the previous model, and the cars can now race for a full hour on one charge. The new batteries also give greater power, increasing the top speed from 225 km/h to 280 km/h. Much of this new technology will make it on to roads in the years to come in new generations of electric production cars.

Cars must race on just one set of tyres.

The chassis is a carbon-fibre and aluminium monocoque.

Rear wheels are covered by aerodynamic 'winglets'.

SPARK GEN2

WEIGHT:
Car (including driver) 900 kg
Battery 385 kg

POWER:
270 hp

TOP SPEED:
280 km/h

0–100 KM/H:
2.8 seconds

TECH POINT

The **powertrain** of a car is the system that converts the energy in the fuel or battery into turning the wheels. In electric cars, electricity from the battery is sent to the motors. The motors contain magnets that spin a rotor when an electric current is applied. The rotors in turn power the wheels.

An LCD display on the steering wheel shows the driver how much power is left in the battery.

GLOSSARY

Acceleration
The rate at which a moving object's velocity is changing. The velocity of an object is its speed and direction of movement.

Aerodynamics
The way in which a gas or liquid moves around a solid object as it passes through it. Engineers study aerodynamics to produce cars with a shape that allows air to move around them smoothly.

Alloy
A material made by mixing two or more metals or by mixing metal with other substances.

Chassis
A strong frame to which the body of a car is attached.

Cylinder
A chamber inside an engine inside which fuel burns to drive a piston up and down and generate power.

Downforce
A force that pushes down on a car to keep it on the road. Parts of a car are designed to generate the right amount of downforce without producing too much drag.

Drag
A force that resists the movement of an object through a gas or liquid. Drag acts in the opposite direction to the direction of the movement, slowing the object down.

Handling
The ease with which a driver can control a car.

Horsepower (hp)
A unit of measurement for power, or the rate at which work is done. One horsepower is roughly equal to the power of one strong horse.

Hybrid
A car that is powered by a petrol engine and one or more electric motors.

Monocoque
A strong exterior shell to a vehicle that provides it with structural support.

Muscle car
A powerful road car with a large engine.

Powertrain
The parts of a car involved in producing and transferring power for the wheels, including the engine or motor, the transmission, drive shafts and wheels.

Roll cage
A strong metal frame that protects the driver in the event of a crash.

Suspension
A system of springs and shock absorbers that connects the wheels of a car to the chassis.

Transmission
The part of a car that transfers power from the engine to the wheels via a gearbox.

Turbine
A machine with blades that spin when a gas or liquid is passed through them.

A SHORT HISTORY OF MOTOR RACING FIRSTS

EVENT	LOCATION	YEAR	WINNER	CAR
First official organised race	Paris to Rouen, France	1894	Albert Lemaître (France)	Peugeot Type 7
First Indy500	Indianapolis, USA	1911	Ray Harroun (USA)	Marmon Wasp
First 24 Hours of Le Mans	Le Mans, France	1923	André Lagache, René Léonard (France)	Chenard-Walcker Type U3
First Monaco Grand Prix	Monte Carlo, Monaco	1929	William Grover-Williams (UK)	Bugatti T35B
First NASCAR race	Charlotte Speedway, USA	1949	Jim Roper (USA)	Lincoln Cosmopolitan
First Formula 1 Grand Prix	Silverstone, England	1950	Giuseppe Farina (Italy)	Alfa Romeo 158
First Official National Hot Rod Association drag race	Great Bend, Kansas	1955	Calvin Rice (USA)	Custom drag racer
First FIA Karting World Championship	Rome, Italy	1964	Guido Sala (Italy)	Tecno kart
First WRC rally	Monte Carlo, Monaco	1973	Jean-Claude Andruet (France)	Alpine Renault A110 1800
First Formula E race	Beijing, China	2014	Lucas di Grassi (Brazil)	Spark-Renault SRT01E

INDEX